A ROOKIE READER®

IF I WERE AN ANT

By Amy Moses

Illustrations by Tom Dunnington

Prepared under the direction of Robert Hillerich, Ph.D.

CHILDRENS PRESS®
CHICAGO

For Heidi, Celia, Joshua, Noah, and Miriam

Library of Congress Cataloging-in-Publication Data

Moses, Amy.
    If I were an ant / by Amy Moses ; illustrated by Tom
Dunnington.
       p.   cm. — (A Rookie reader)
    Summary: A child imagines how much larger things
such as crumbs, puddles, trees, and even babies would
seem to an ant.
    ISBN 0-516-02011-0
    [1. Ants—Fiction. 2. Size—Fiction.] I. Dunnington,
Tom, ill. II. Title. III. Series.
PZ7.M84698If   1992
[E]—dc20   92-12947
                               CIP
                               AC

If I were an ant,
a meadow would be a jungle.

If I were an ant,
a crack would be a crater.

6

If I were an ant,
a pebble would be a mountain.

If I were an ant,

a breeze would be a hurricane.

If I were an ant,
a raindrop would be a flood.

11

If I were an ant,
a puddle would be an ocean.

13

If I were an ant,
a blade of grass would be a tree.

If I were an ant,
a flower would be an umbrella.

If I were an ant,
a tree would be a skyscraper.

If I were an ant,
a baby would be a giant.

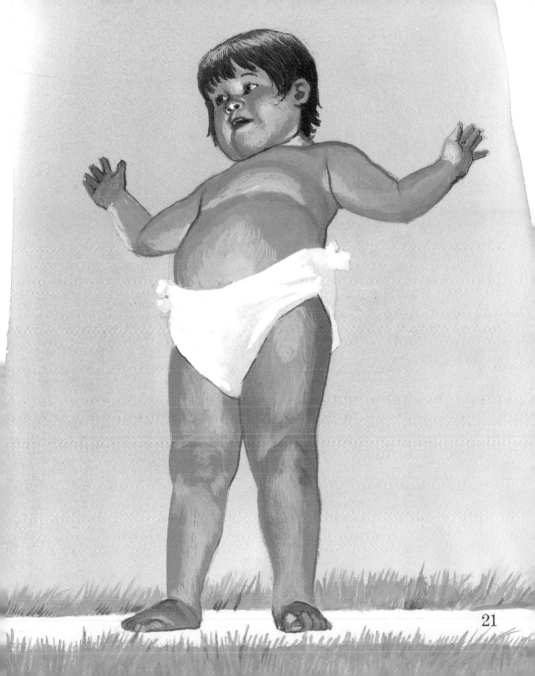

22

If I were an ant,
a crumb would be a feast.

If I were an ant,
an anthill would be a palace.

If I were an ant,
the world would seem
even bigger to me than
it does now!

If I were an ant,
would I wonder what it would
be like to be a person?

What do you think?

WORD LIST

a	does	me	than
an	even	meadow	the
ant	feast	mountain	think
anthill	flood	now	to
baby	flower	ocean	tree
be	giant	of	umbrella
bigger	grass	palace	were
blade	hurricane	pebble	what
breeze	I	person	wonder
crack	if	puddle	world
crater	it	raindrop	would
crumb	jungle	seem	you
do	like	skyscraper	

About the Author

Amy Moses is an aunt! She has five nieces and nephews. They are the children to whom this book is dedicated. She enjoys reading and telling stories to them, and of course pretending. Playing make-believe with her nieces and nephews gave her the idea for this book.

About the Artist

Tom Dunnington divides his time between book illustrations and wildlife painting. He has done many books for Childrens Press, as well as working on textbooks, and is a regular contributor to "Highlights for Children." Tom lives in Oak Park, Illinois.